Prosperity, Plenitude & *Infinite* Possibilities

Michael B. Beckwith
Founder & Spiritual Director
Agape International Spiritual Center

TABLE OF CONTENTS

INTRODUCTION

Welcome to *Prosperity, Plenitude & Infinite Possibilities*, the companion book/journal to the class I have taught at Agape International which contains core teachings on prosperity. It is my privilege to share this with you.

When people think of prosperity, they often think of financial wealth, material items, and acquiring whatever the latest gadget or toy that's currently trending. However, true prosperity is a spiritual principle governed by the spiritual laws that imbue our very lives. It is state of mind and heart, an awareness, and an absolute knowing that we live and breathe in a field of infinite possibilities that meets all of our needs each and every time. That we are all endowed with the spiritual, mental, emotional, and material means to share our unique gifts and talents in the world to the degree that we are open to the perpetual flow of good that surrounds us. We come to learn that with everything we've been taught around scarcity, lack, and not enough-ness, that we must struggle, fight, manipulate, and compete with each other just to get our sliver of this ever-decreasing finite pie, *is simply not true.* Prosperity is, in truth, who and what we are.

Just like the air we breathe yet can't see, and the law of gravity which we experience but whose mechanisms we can't see, the universal laws that govern all life, including prosperity, operate in the same way. It surrounds us although we may not see it or its mechanisms. However, unlike oxygen and gravity which operate in spite of what we may believe, our thoughts, beliefs, and feelings, conditioned by what we've been taught, actually determines how prosperity flows to us.

As the saying goes, "God doesn't provide the vision without the provision." Those familiar with my teachings know that God is not some anthropomorphic being in the sky, but is an omnipotent, omniscient, and omnipresent ineffable field that permeates our very being. It's a presence that is never an absence. As we come to grasp and grok that understanding as a way of living and being, life opens up for us in miraculous ways.

THE PURPOSE OF THIS BOOK

This book is based on the live transcript of my *Prosperity, Plenitude & Infinite Possibilities* class, and is designed as a prayer, reference, practice, and activation manual. You are here to activate your innate spiritual capacities and abilities. You are here to evoke the inherent spiritual qualities of prosperity, plenitude, love, beauty, joy, creativity, generosity, and compassion so that they may express themselves fully and freely in your life. The exercises, prayers, affirmations, and contemplative meditations will entrain your mind and nervous system to dismantle the limited perceptions of the human condition, and align your awareness with spiritual truth and the reality of love.

Get ready to shine!

Peace & Richest Blessings,
Michael B. Beckwith
Founder & Spiritual Director
Agape International Spiritual Center

iv

Welcome to your

Infinite
Possibilities

ACTIVATION OF THE SACRED TRUTH

Prosperity, Plenitude & Infinite Possibilities is about the activation of that which is sacred within us.   We are not simply having a cerebral understanding of what prosperity is and the laws around it. We are activating that which allows us to be the vehicle through which prosperity can manifest within us with ease and grace so that the struggle many of us have around prosperity begins to dissolve.

When we speak about prosperity, we're speaking about having all of our legitimate needs met.   We use the word legitimate because there are certain things that people have considered or believed to be needs that are not necessarily so. There's a lot of immature wanting that goes on in this consumer-driven materialistic society. But within us all is an awareness of what it feels like to have all our needs met without struggle.   In his sermon on the mount, Jesus said, that the lilies of the field spin and toil not, so do not have one anxious thought about how you shall clothe or feed yourself. This "lilies-of-the-field" consciousness, this vibration of all needs met, is what we want to carry.

You want to carry around the thought and feeling that all of your needs are met so that's where you begin to live from, think from, prepare from, act from, speak from, and have your conversations from, and that the fear, anxiety, and worry that move through the field of human consciousness on a regular basis does not direct your conversation or your actions.

When we use the word "field," we understand that there is a magnetic and gravitational field that of course cannot be seen by or touched with the physical senses, but they affect us nevertheless. There are also fields of belief, and fields of experience that are generated by conversation and belief. Therefore, in a spiritual community, we're seeking to be conscious of that. Not as hypothesis or conjecture, but as really living, moving, and having our being in the field of the Presence which is never an absence. This Presence, by whatever name you choose to call it—Divine love, Divine life, pure intelligence, God—is everywhere, and to the degree that it becomes an activity of our awareness, we enter into this lilies-of-the-field consciousness where all of our needs are met without having to think about it.

Now you do live in the lilies-of-the-field consciousness in certain areas of your life. For example, you woke up this morning and your heart was beating. You didn't do some heavy affirmations to get it jump-started. You didn't pray to God, *"Please, I want my heart to beat today."* You also didn't say, *"God, I ate some food last night. Can you please help me digest it?"* No, you basically live in the field of God, and on your subjective and subconscious level of awareness, there's activity going on at the neurovegetative and physical level that is digesting your food, eliminating toxins, and turning that energy into bone, sinew, and muscle. All of that is happening right now without you having to think about it. Now you can think about it or pray about it if you want, but for the most part, it's happening at the lilies-of-the-field consciousness vibration on a subconscious level.

What we're seeking to do is extend that subconscious yes-to-life vibration into every area of our life, just like when you cut yourself accidentally and the body immediately begins to mend itself. You clean the wound and the body begins to heal because there's a subconscious agreement around the body mending and repairing itself. So in the same sense, as we begin to eliminate the toxic thoughts and beliefs around prosperity and abundance and embrace on a subconscious level the activation of these sacred truths, we can begin to demonstrate—just as our food digests without any help from our conscious mind—our needs being needs met in an ever-increasing capacity without us consciously trying to make it happen. There's an utter yielding, surrendering, and allowing vibration that lets this happen.

As you dedicate yourself to activating these sacred truths, you'll begin to notice the arguments within yourself that fights against your Self, as well as the patterns you've picked up that delay and deny this activity. And you'll also come to fully embrace that it's okay to be prosperous, to have all of your needs met, and to swim in a field of abundance without feeling bad.

Coming into the understanding that to be a beneficial Presence on the planet means we must carry a certain vibration, it also means taking on your incarnation fully and embodying these sacred truths so that whatever is your particular task or assignment for your life, you're able to move into it enthusiastically without the fear of not having everything you need. Without the fear of this belief dragging you through life and preventing you from living your life according to the Divine plan and sacred agreement you made with yourself before your soul incarnated on this planet, you begin to release the brakes and allow it to be okay.

Michael B. Beckwith

I AM AND I HAVE

Many years ago when Agape was at its previous Santa Monica location, there was a group of us who liked to meet at Agape and go bike-riding early in the morning. I considered myself to be in pretty good shape at the time, and tended to ride faster than some in our group. But one morning during our bike ride, I noticed that a lot of people were passing me by, even those who normally rode several paces behind me. While they were breezing past me, I was huffing and puffing trying to keep up and figure out what the heaven was going on with me. As we got back to Agape, I was in last place. Then I realized, as I stopped the bicycle, that I had been riding the entire time with my brakes on!

Of course, I was very much relieved to discover this. But this was definitely a living metaphor for us as human beings who are surrounded by a field of plenitude, abundance, beauty, and infinite possibilities yet walk through this life with the mental and emotional brakes of our beliefs, conversations, and actions on therefore hindering the full flow of Spirit from expressing through us. We want to start looking at and dissolving those brakes and the ways in which we hold ourselves captive to limited paradigms and points of view so that we consciously, vibrationally live, think, and act from *I am and I have.*

I am and I have is not merely about what we can see with our senses, it's the ability to participate and play in the realm of what we *can't see*. That which is real, that which is forever and eternal, and that which is of abundance and plenitude, is invisible. Now this may be a difficult thing for you to capture because when we think about prosperity, wealth, and abundance, we think about money, material items, and having the latest gadget, toy, or whatever new hot item is trending. But prosperity has its genesis in the unseen. Individuals who are growing and unfolding spiritually by touching their Divine nature while living in this human incarnation are learning to hold themselves accountable by living in the awareness of the unseen, and being the conduit through which the unseen becomes visible as their life, as their legitimate needs being met, and as whatever they need to show up in life to carry out their particular task or assignment, be it money, ideal employment, or opportunities, but its genesis is in the ever-expanding awareness of that which can never be seen by the senses.

Now when we *really* catch this, we get to play in this Invisible Infinite **every single day as the new starting point for our life**, not the issues and problems we may have to face in the course of the day, and not the pictures of what we don't have and what we don't want. We start from the realm of what we can't see, and we begin to develop an activation of a feeling tone of *I am and I have* and all needs met.

Michael B. Beckwith

CRAZY VIBRATIONAL INTENTIONALITY

I want you to do this now: bring your awareness from your head and into your heart. Consider something you want your life to be about that appears impossible for you to do, accomplish, or have. Think of something outrageous! Free your mind from the present paradigm in which you're living, and begin to see yourself being about that thing, doing that thing that's totally outrageous to your mind. Think about the kind of money you want to have, the kind of gift and contribution you want to give to the world, the kind of business you want to establish, the way you want to walk on the planet right now if you were uninhibited by your present paradigm, circumstances, conditions, conditioning, and opinions of yourself. What would that look like?

Notice that as I'm telling you this, the mind

is trying to tell you to be "reasonable." The mind is saying, *"I really want to have it but...."* No, let your mind go crazy for a moment because we want to break free from the paradigm in which we are living. We want to come into the field of possibility and the miraculous. Begin to think about something about your life. And don't consider, *OMG, if this really happens, what's going to happen to everybody else? What's everybody else going to think about me if I suddenly get or become a _____ (fill-in-the-blank)? How's it going to affect everybody else if I suddenly have all of my needs met and I begin to live like this, share, contribute, build, and have?* No, don't think about the considerations. Think about the feeling tone of living beyond your present paradigm right now.

Now take a breath, hold for 10 seconds, and contemplate letting your mind break free from the present way of thinking and begin to see yourself living full-on. There is vitality, vigor, strength, harmonizing prosperity, wealth, and abundance. There's no consideration of a seeming lack of resources, no seeming lack of opportunities, no seeming lack of support in any area of your life— all of this is a given. You have everything you need. Now start to see yourself being what you are called to be on this planet at this time in human history, and begin to just allow the mystic cord of memory that connects you to the eternal before you had this human incarnation. You're beginning to remember that you are a singular manifestation of a cosmic good that's unfolding to reflect and reveal the eternal. That you are to have this earthly incarnation but your true home is the cosmos and you've limited yourself temporarily to put inhibitors on and have a limited point of view. You're breaking free from that right now. Break free from any limiting paradigms right now. Can you see yourself living the life, having the feeling tone of a life of abundance, plenitude, prosperity, and all needs met? See yourself living that life now. All needs met is the starting point of your life.

Now as you feel[1] into this, take a deep breath, hold for 10 seconds, then release. Let this now be an intention. Not, *I'm going to make this happen.* Not willfulness, but a willingness, to live life at this vibratory frequency. Intention offers a vibrational direction, and means you're willing to live life at this level.

---

1. There's a difference between emotion and feeling. Emotion is the sub-strata of previously held points of view which, whether they're true or not, becomes part of your emotional body. Feeling is a direct contact with the sacred qualities and is how we connect to God.

We're not considering how will this happen. We're considering breaking free from our limited paradigm. Now something the mind would say right now is, *"This is crazy! No, this is damn near impossible! How could I accomplish that? I'm too old. I don't have enough resources. It's too late in life. I don't have enough preparation. No, no, no, it's crazy! This is crazy-making! No, I can't!"*

But yes, *you can!* Yes, you can let it be. As you allow these seed ideas to escape the paradigm of your limited point of view, you are now giving yourself permission to let this be an intention. A direction. Now give yourself permission to feel into the sacred qualities underlying this life, accomplishments, and contributions, qualities such as genius activation, love, beauty, generosity, compassion, creativity, joy, bliss, and ecstasy. Allow these eternal, spiritual qualities to break free in you. Remember, you are a singular manifestation of a cosmic good that is forever unfolding. These spiritual qualities are seeking to release themselves through you and the life you want to live. In fact, the life you want to live is the vehicle for these qualities. You're surrounded by abundance. Do not limit these sacred qualities by constraining yourself to a little life. Do not drive with your brakes on!

A DIRECTIONAL WILLINGNESS AND INTENTION

L et's go through this again as this bears frequent repeating. Whenever the mind thinks that something you desire is just too big, too much, too crazy, or says, *"I don't know how to accomplish it,"* just let your imagination run wild with seeing yourself living a life full of abundance, plenitude, and prosperity with all needs met. This is a stretch exercise. It can even seem somewhat immature with some of the things you want to accomplish. You might even feel a little embarrassed by it. But you don't have to share it with anybody right now, just keep it to yourself. And as you say, *"I'm going to live full out and this is what it looks like,"* this becomes your starting point.

This is beyond what you can do by yourself. You have to have Divine intervention. There has to be a miracle. There has to be support. There has to be something else working with you and on your behalf for this to occur. Now just be with that for a second. As Henry David Thoreau reminded us, *as we begin to walk in the direction of a life beyond what we can even imagine now, unseen laws come into place.* Things begin to occur for us that otherwise could not take place until we had that kind of intentionality and willingness. Now begin to notice what spiritual, eternal qualities are underneath this willingness to live this life. Is it love, beauty, joy, harmony, creativity, bliss, ecstasy, happiness, etc.? Feel into that in this instant.

Take a deep breath, hold for 10 seconds, release, and feel into it. Feel into the mind stretching beyond its present border. Feel into the intentionality that's a willingness, not willfulness. Feel into the sacred qualities that are seeking to emerge.

Now, consider a moment in your life where you actually felt that all of your needs were met. If you do not remember a time in your life where all your needs were met, just imagine what would it feel like if you had no worries and all of your needs were met.

Tap into that mystical memory. Tap into when there were no anxious thoughts about the future. It wasn't, *okay my needs are met this minute, but how am I going to make it tomorrow or next week?* No, not that, but an awareness that your needs were met and that's just where you lived. It was grace. It was Garden-of-Eden consciousness. It was Shangri-La. Heaven. Remember that moment and let it be active in you right now.

The mind is now stretched beyond the present paradigm of what we think is possible. Take a deep breath. Hold for 10 seconds. Release. We are establishing an intention, a directional willingness, to live this life. We're not asking how we're going to do this. We're establishing ourselves as a field of living intelligence. Feel that intention. Take a deep breath. Hold for 10 seconds. Release.

Now give yourself permission to let your intuition guide you into what qualities are seeking to emerge through a life lived by spiritual design. Not by the default system of societal thought-forms, parental fantasies of who they think you should be, or the fears about your life. But a life designed from the mind of God. Notice what bubbles up for you. What inherent spiritual qualities are seeking to be activated and expressed in the course of this life that you're here to live? Take a breath around that. Hold it for 10 seconds. Release.

Let's build upon this exercise.

Now recall a moment in which all of your needs were met. I say recall because there's a difference between recall and memory. Memory is oftentimes connected with the brain and neurovegetative systems, recall is from the soul. Sometimes physically you may forget something or lose your memory around certain things, but you never lose your recall because it is a spiritual faculty which your soul never forgets. So when you recall a moment in which all of your needs were met, you're recalling a dimension of your own spiritual nature. This is where the worry and anxiety that becomes a part of our braking system didn't exist because they weren't activated. We were free, we were creative, we had all needs met.

Feel into that. Take a deep breath, hold for 10 seconds, multiply that feeling times 10, then release the breath. Feel into the feeling tone of all needs met. Take a deep breath, hold for 10 seconds, multiply that feeling times 50, then release the breath. *All needs met. All needs met. All needs met. All needs met.* Take a deep breath, hold for 10 seconds, multiply the feeling times 100, then release the breath. Take another deep breath, multiply the feeling of all needs met times 1,000, release the breath. This is how we exponentially increase our awareness around the feeling tonality that all of our needs met. Take another breath, feel all needs met times 1,000, then hold the breath hold for 10 seconds. *You are the light. The light that lights up every man and woman that comes unto the world. All of your needs are met. Everything is working together for your good. Worry, doubt, and fear are dissolved.* Now, release the breath. Here are your four entry points or domains that are now activated to a greater degree:

1. A life beyond what you can presently imagine.

2. An expansion of the perceptual paradigm.

3. Directional willingness and intention.

4. Spiritual qualities and all needs met as the starting point.

Michael B. Beckwith

LOCKING IN THE FEELING TONE OF ALL NEEDS MET

Now expand your awareness and feel yourself into a moment of recalling the Divine celebration of merely existing. Celebrate yourself for merely existing without attaching any story to it. We have so many stories of blame and shame, as well as stories of reward, that modulate our happiness. We feel happy when we like a story, and unhappy when we don't like the story. But for now, enter into the feeling tone of celebration, recalling what it is to celebrate your existence. Now, all four domains are active right here. Enter into the field of celebration. Free yourself!

Let's lock in this vibration with an activation exercise called The Morter March developed by my dear friend, Master of Bio-Energetic Medicine and Quantum Field visionary, Dr. Sue Morter. Remember, understanding prosperity is more than a cerebral exercise, it's activating the quality of prosperity that's seeking to emerge through you your life. The Morter March is a daily practice that helps us to integrate whatever we're trying to embody more easily, rapidly, and efficiently. For a visual reference, please watch this short video at Dr. Sue's website: https://drsuemorter.com/morter-march-mpower-step/

Here's how to do The Morter March[2]:

1. Stand with your feet hip-width apart and your spine straight and tall.

2. Take a step forward with your right leg and bend your right knee in a lunge so you can feel your right thigh muscles activate. Let your conscious awareness drop down into your body.

3. Raise your left arm in front of you, pointed at a 45-degree angle toward where the ceiling and wall meet. Turn your palm so your thumb is pointing upward.

4. Extend your right arm back and down behind you at a 45-degree angle, toward where the

2. Morter, Sue, DC. *The Energy Codes: The 7-Step System to Awaken Your Spirit, Heal Your Body, and Live Your Best Life.* New York: Atria Books, 2019. Pages 161-162

wall meets the floor. Point the thumb down. Extend your fingers to enliven them.

5. Tilt and slightly turn your head to the left and look directly up your left arm to your left thumb. Close your right eye.

6. Now, standing in this position, take a deep belly breath and hold it. Focus on a deep sense of well-being, or the feeling of forgiveness, acceptance, and love. (Feel into your intention and the spiritual qualities it represents, and recall all needs met).

7. Retain the breath until you can no longer hold it, or about the time it takes to slowly count to 10.

8. Exhale then step back to center with your feet parallel and hip-width apart.

9. Repeat on the left side, then once more on each side, for a total of four repetitions. The more you do this clearing code exercise, the more shifts you will start to see.

Your mind is now breaking free of any limiting paradigm. You're aware you're giving birth in this dimension to spiritual qualities that are inherent within us all, and you're recalling what it feels like to have all needs met. Anxiety is dissolved. Fear is gone.

When you have completed this exercise, bring your hands together into a prayerful mudra with this prayer:

And it is from this awareness, feeling, and sensing that there is only one Being here revealing the one power, the one Presence, and the one life that I give vent to with such thanksgiving and gratitude, such pure appreciation for existence itself, and that this word serves as a law of elimination to any thought-forms or mental patterning that becomes emotional patterning of lack and limitation, scarcity and not enoughness, and allows us to soar on the wings of the Holy Spirit, that we may be the vehicles through which more life and more love, beauty, abundance, joy, wealth, wellness, well-being, and harmonizing prosperity can reveal itself with an ease and a grace without struggle. Nothing in us in this moment denies the great possibilities that lie within us all. Everything within us is a "yes" and amen and we feel it in our bones that everything is working together for our good, and that this united state of consciousness that has been established is a field, a rich field of infinite potential, Divine possibilities, and that we feel it's all right. It's all right to be prosperous. It's all right to have all of our needs met. It's all right to make major contributions to the world. It's all right to be generous. It's all right to be creative. It's all right to live above mere survival. We break free from the limited paradigm of not enoughness and scarcity and stand in the awareness that if God is for us, there can be no thing against us. This is what we feel in our bones and we call forth the health, the well-being, the Divine prosperity, and the wellness that takes over our life right now. We feel it. And we give thanks for it. And so it is. Amen.

Once again, take a deep breath. Hold it for 10 seconds while every cell in your body absorbs this, and the neurovegetative and nervous systems acclimate around this frequency, beyond thinkingness. This is an awareness that all of our needs are met. Release the breath. Take another deep breath, and release the sound of OM. Now feel into the silence, into that space where the OM just was. *Everything that is comes from no thing.* Take a deep breath and release the sound of OM. *Everything that is comes from no thing, the realm of the invisible.* Feel into the space where the OM was. Take a deep breath, release the OM, then feel into the silence. *Everything that is, everything that manifests comes from that which is unmanifest. The Source. The substance that is invisible. Amen.*

SPIRITUAL DISCERNMENT

We begin with this opening prayer:

And so as we continue to give thanks for this sweet day, affirming the truth of our own being, that each of us are becoming living affirmations of that which is real, that which is eternal and, that which is forever, and allow ourselves to be a generative field of abundance, a generative field of harmonizing prosperity, a generative field of wealth and well-being, and a deep intrinsic feeling tonality of all of our needs met being the activity of our awareness, we just give great thanks to the great God of the Universe that's everywhere in its fullness and that by means of us gets to express Itself more completely and more fully, that anything that would hinder, delay, obstruct, or deny this, we're giving ourselves permission to shake it off, to release it so that the obscurations of the mind are disintegrated as we become more integrated with who and what we really are. Who being an individual expression of the what, the what being the indivisible invisible Presence that has no beginning and will never end, and so we become firmly established men and women in this dynamic Presence, and for this we take a vibrational stand in gratitude, thanksgiving, appreciation. We let it be now and unto forever more. And so it is. And so we are. And so I AM. Amen.

Take a deep breath, hold for 10 seconds, then release. We are generating a rich and powerful field around all of our needs met. We're generating a field around wealth and abundance, around appreciation and gratitude, around harmonizing prosperity, and we're living, moving, and having our being in it.

So to recap what we've done so far: we have expanded our point of view, perception, and paradigm by thinking of something outrageous that we don't know how to do so that the *how* doesn't interfere before we get into the feeling tone of the *what*. Next, we established our intention and expanded our awareness of the spiritual qualities of prosperity and abundance so that they become the government under which we live. Then we recalled what it feels like to have all needs met and entrained our mind and nervous system around that truth.

It's worth noting that on a soul level, on a deeply spiritual level, you know that all of your needs are met. However, you've gotten caught in the undertow of the human experiential domain and therefore see life through that perception. This generates emotions and defense mechanisms around that, as well as protective ways of being in the world, including immature wanting and acquisitive thinking. This is why we recalled the *I AM and I have* spiritual faculty and activated it through contemplation and prayer to generate the feeling tone of all needs met.

The domain of plenitude and abundance is the field in which we live. However, we have subconscious and even conscious filters through which we see that determines our perception, conversation, decision-making, actions, and choices. And so we want to have a level of spiritual discernment so that we're able to tell the difference between whether we're operating through a filter or the truth.

In our society there are many filters that have become gross and normalized. For instance, the wealth gap between the haves and the have-nots is a discussion that dominates our society and world.

A belief in scarcity and lack has activated in people an acquisitive nature where they just want and get, and has generated a field of scarcity that exacerbated itself into this wealth gap. This then creates an ever-increasing emotional tone and experience of lack, scarcity, and not enough-ness. These filters become experience. We see it in the news media, in our socioeconomic policies, systems and structures, and we see people experiencing lack, homelessness, and similar things. So our senses are bombarded with the thought-form of not enough-ness, even though we know that in reality there's more than enough for everyone. In reality, we know that we live in a sea of abundance and plenitude, but the filters of separation have produced this gross experience for many people. And so you have to think outside of that filter, outside your present paradigm, even as you're presented with physical evidence of thought-forms of lack and limitation.

To do this, there has to be a simultaneous awareness of compassion. When we see the gross evidence of not enough-ness, we know on a spiritual level it's a filter that someone has gotten caught up in, or that someone is taking on that particular incarnation for the elevation of compassion. So there has to be spiritual discernment, and there has to be an opting out of that paradigm. And when we opt out of that paradigm, we become candidates for the ineffable Presence that is never detoured, denied, or delayed, and does not get its power from any physical condition. Abundance, plenitude, and prosperity are all spiritual qualities that are not governed by conditions of the world, so you're in the process of discerning a filter that may be running you and pulling yourself out of it. Just like prosperity and abundance, you're not governed by the filters of the world.

This is Prosperity 101: your good does not come from a present condition being a certain way. This doesn't mean that in the human world you don't work, lobby, or vote to change conditions and make things better for people. You absolutely can and should. But what I'm saying is that the genesis of prosperity and abundance, health and well-being, and all of the spiritual qualities are not determined by condition, but by consciousness. This is where the rubber hits the road. Are you willing to be discerning of a condition without being caught up in it?

Discernment is a spiritual faculty that allows you to tell the difference between that which is real and that which is transitory. You're not just committing a spiritual lobotomy by saying, *"Well everything is all good"* without discerning that there's some things that aren't good or are destructive. But, you have the power of discernment. This means that this condition and situation is temporary and not valid because it's not in tune with the fundamental harmony of the Universe. And you're able to tell the difference without judgment. That's discernment.

Now beyond discernment is something called beholding, where we're absolutely able to see the Presence everywhere. That's where we're able to say, *"All is good."* You don't give up your discernment, but you're able to see that which is valid and invalid occupy the same space and still see that all is well. This is not a spiritual bypass, it's an ability to see that the Presence is right in the midst of what appears to be a limiting condition. In the field of plenitude, you become aware of your filters. When you look at the news, you can see what filters you get caught up in. What gets you angry, and what cherished opinions you have.

You may say, *"But oh, there's the haves and the have-nots!"* or *"There are some evil people around and they're doing all these evil things."* I am not saying this is untrue. We could call them evil, or we could just say they're ignorant, unenlightened, uninitiated, unevolved, fearful, scared, scarred, or various combinations thereof that would have people accumulate, acquire, or manipulate so that they have more, while other people have less.

You're able to see what filters you're caught up in so that you can consciously come back to *God is all there is.* It's a vibrational stand where you know you're going to manifest and demonstrate not from a change in condition, but from a change in perception. We shift our consciousness through our activation exercises, which allows us to hold that perception.

FREE YOURSELF FROM UNFORGIVENESS

Another way to help us think outside of our filters and to shift our perception is through the practice of forgiveness. **When unforgiveness operates in our heart, we signal to the Universe that someone owes us something**. That's our message. This person did me wrong. This person did not do the right thing and therefore, what they did or did not do is determining my destiny. So the law I have now evoked is, *I don't have something because someone owes me something*.

How does that spin out in the world? That spins out as debt. Debt is a function of unforgiveness and the belief that someone owes you something. I'm not saying that people haven't done things to you, stolen things from you, or may owe you money or stuff. I'm not saying that that's not valid. What I am saying here is that *you have a choice as to where you're going to live your life.* Are you going to live in a state of constant consternation, or are you going to free yourself and move into the field that eliminates the filter of lack, limitation, scarcity, and unforgiveness?

You have a choice where this is concerned and when you choose to extricate yourself from the vibration of the gross expression of scarcity and unforgiveness, what happens is that you get to begin your life anew. You're in that world, but not of it. You're in the world, but you're on another frequency.

Take a deep breath and exhale. Contemplate what filters have snagged you. Is it the anger around the rising inequality? Is it a thought-form that there really isn't enough to go around? Is it that somebody has done you wrong and you're never going to be able to turn your life around? Is it any one of these things, or your own unique version of those thoughts? Notice the filter, because filters can become an excuse, a hardened perception, and where we think from.

But to extricate ourselves from and override these filters, we have to think from the invisible *I AM and I have.* Inhale, *We have to think from the invisible.* Exhale, *I am absolutely connected with the Presence.* Inhale, *We have to think from the invisible.*

Exhale, *Everything I need, want, hope for, and desire, I already have.* Inhale, *We have to think from the invisible.* Exhale, *Everything is working together for my good even though I can't see it.*

Notice any filters that seem so legitimate that you're now willing to let go of. Now letting go of these filters does not mean you're letting people off the hook or pretending that something didn't happen a certain way. You're taking yourself out of that little world of unforgiveness, scarcity, and lack because plenitude and abundance is where you really live, move, and have your being, but it must have access through your awareness.

Give yourself permission to see the Presence of abundance right here, right now, even in the world. We can see and discern the gross experience of limitation and scarcity in self-aggrandizement and greed when we see pollution in the ocean and toxicity in the soil. We can see and discern misguided thinking in avarice and greed when we see the diminishment of species in rain forests. We can discern all of that, but there's a healing going on. A healing coming back into our awareness that beyond the gross expression of a limited point of view, there is something that needs no condition to bring into expression more good through us. As we see and discern the filters, we give ourselves permission to behold the Presence and we begin with our own mind. Notice the filters and be willing to drop them, not from discernment, but from being active in us. It's a dispassionate yet compassionate way of looking at the world.

It's like if a great paramedic rushed to the scene of an accident and saw someone bleeding. They don't deny that the person is bleeding, nor do they ask why is this person bleeding and whose fault it is. They instantly know exactly how to stop the bleeding, and to say the right things that bring about a level of calm and comfort to the patient, thereby creating the vibrational condition for mending and healing. It's discernment to see the both wound and the blood, then to see the wholeness and how to allow that to manifest.

What filters have you snagged? Is it something you inherited from your parents around money? Is it that money is illusive? Is it that money is hard to get? Is it that there is not enough money? Are all rich people bad people? Is anyone who has their needs met evil? Is there some unforgiveness that's operating in your heart that would have you make a demand on the Universe that only you could demand of yourself? Notice the filter and be willing to let it go and to think from another domain. What is that domain? *That God is all there is. Life is for me and not against me. All of my needs are met. I am becoming the rich vibrational condition through which the Infinite Invisible can begin to express itself. What needs to change, must first change within me.*

The debt that's been accumulated, has been accumulated through unforgiveness. If you're holding unforgiveness towards those who talked about you, those who fired you, those who let you go, those who didn't quite understand you, those whom you thought didn't appreciate your gifts and talents, those whom you think owe you something, you're saying to the Universe, *am I missing something?* Then the experience becomes you're missing something and therefore are not having something, and it becomes an endless cycle.

We want to give up the endless for that which is eternal. So, are you willing to be whole? Are you willing to be free? Are you willing to be prosperous? Are you willing to be wealthy? Are you willing to be a great steward of wealth? Are you willing to be a great steward of prosperity? Are you willing to be more? Are you willing to release the filters here and now?

Feel into this and repeat:

I am available to more good than I've ever imagined!

I am available to more good than I've ever imagined, experienced, or manifested!

I am available to more prosperity than I've ever imagined!

I am available to more prosperity than I've ever experienced!

I am available to more prosperity than I've ever manifested!

I am going beyond my present paradigm!

Beyond my imagination!

Beyond my previous experience!

Beyond my previous manifestations!

Feel into that.

Our good is not based upon anything we've ever done vibrationally. There's no preset condition needed other than in our own awareness for the onslaught and expression of the eternal. Say, *"Here today, prosperity, harmonizing prosperity! Here today, abundance! Here today, wealth and well-being!"* We're pressing the reset button here. We live in a field of plenitude.

Take a deep breath, hold for 10 seconds, exhale, and contemplate seeing plenitude. Notice infinity or the representation of infinity in the manifest world. Notice the infinite amount of leaves on trees. Notice the infinite amount of foliage and flowers. Notice the infinite grains of sand on the beach. Notice the infinite blades of grass shooting up from the earth (even when grass is cut down it continues to grow). Notice all the beings, fingerprints, and hair—no two are the same. Everything is unique, even in the same species. This is God's infinite nature. Feel yourself in the flow of infinity. Feel scarcity, lack, and limitation yielding to infinity, plenitude, and abundance.

As you go through the course of your day, give yourself permission to ask yourself where am I thinking from? The Infinite? The plenitude, or the limited? The manifestation of the Infinite is a spiritual hook-up with the Presence that's right here in you. It's an inherent field of plenitude.

Yes, there are filters of separation, scarcity, lack, and limitation that have become the gross experience leading to avarice, greed, and manipulation on one hand, or unworthiness on the other. However, *the genesis of your abundance is in your own heart and mind today.* In this beginning, God. In this beginning, love. In this beginning, abundance. In this beginning, plenitude. In this beginning, all needs met. The good you seek to manifest is from the invisible yet indivisible realm. Take a deep breath, hold for 10 seconds, then release.

Now just take a moment and bring anyone or anything to mind that needs to be forgiven. See the being or the condition in front of you. Or it can be a symbol of the condition. Say to this being, condition, or symbol, *"You can no longer determine my destiny. You have no power over my destiny. I set you free. I cut the emotional cords."* See in your mind's eye a golden pair of scissors. Say, *"I cut the cords. You're free. I am free. I forgive."*

Something new has now been set in motion. The good that we are seeking to manifest and express is coming directly from the invisible, not from other people, though they may be the channel. It's not coming from any condition, though a certain condition may show up to be the vehicle. It's coming directly from our connection with the Presence. Be bold enough in this instant to claim your connection with the invisible Presence in this field of plenitude. The condition has no power over you. The other beings and people have no power over you. You are at one with all power. All good is from the Presence. People are channels of the good.

Take a deep breath, hold for 10 seconds, and release. Take another deep breath and hold for 10 seconds. You're in contact with the field of plenitude and abundance. This is the beginning point of your life. The forgiveness is continued until there's no emotional reaction to the person or condition. You're not living a life of debt, but a life of freedom. Now release the breath.

This is a field that we are creating around prosperity, plenitude, and abundance. Remember your subconscious awareness of harmonizing prosperity, all needs met, lilies-of-the-field consciousness, ease and grace, and everything working together for your good. Accept that you're living in a field of plenitude, and that although you're in the world, you've now entered into the field of great possibilities.

Michael B. Beckwith

THERE'S GREAT POSSIBILITIES FOR ALL OF US

The spiritual truth is that everything you can want, hope for, and desire, you already have. The spiritual and eternal truth is that you're living in a field of abundance. You can never be ever separated from that. You can experience something other than abundance, but in reality, you can never be separated from it. It's closer than your breath, nearer than your hands and feet.

I want you to consider that incessant thought, that virus, that says over and over that I don't have enough. Maybe it's, *"I don't have enough money. I don't have enough opportunity. I don't have enough prosperity. I'm not creative enough. I don't have enough joy."* Or you may think, *that person or those people are always ideally employed, that person is very creative, those people or that person is very prosperous. Opportunities always surround them.* Whatever that thought is, just be aware of it. Just discern that thought, just discern that virus of the mind. You don't have to agree with it, you don't have to embrace it, just know that it's there.

Now, activate the truth by thinking about at least one person you know—a family member, friend, associate, colleague—who manifests those qualities that the virus of the mind thinks is lacking in you. When you see this person you say, *"Oh wow, they demonstrate prosperity so easily!"* or *"They're so healthy,"* or *"Opportunities just come to them all the time. Good things are always happening to them."* Just think about that person right now. Now as you have this being in your mind, consider this: *you can only see that which is in you.* You can only see what you are projecting onto another. So if you can see abundance, plenitude, creativity, joy, love, etc. in that person, then you are looking at them with the vibration of those qualities. It may be incipient in you. It may be not fully activated, not fully orbed, but you're still seeing it in another which means it has to be somewhat active in you.

The first thing I want you to do is to own it. I want you to embrace that what you're looking at in that other being you're actually projecting it onto them.

And that prosperity, that generation of opportunities, that beauty, that joy—all of that that you see in that being, is a projection from you. You're not taking anything away from them because it's active in them as well, but you could only see it if it was in you. We start there and then as we look at this being, I want you to move into the dynamic of being so grateful that they have what they have. Begin to celebrate what they've got. Give them a standing ovation! Say, *"Thank you for being prosperous! Thank you for being healthy! Thank you for being rich! Thank you for showing me what it looks like! Thank you for being beautiful! Thank you for being creative! Thank you for manifesting good! I'm so happy for you! I'm so happy! Thank you, thank you, thank you!"*

Now, as you're feeling grateful that they're demonstrating what appears to be lacking in us, we are simultaneously breaking free from the ego's perception that says, if good is happening over there, there's less good over here. That's an egoic perception of lack, and it's a lie. If some good is happening anywhere, if someone breaks through and is prosperous, healthy, successful, has been healed of something, or whatever the case may be, it creates a vortex of evolution for everyone to come unto that same frequency. We applaud individuals who are successful, healthy, beautiful, and abundant! We thank them for showing it, for being willing to break free from mediocrity. We thank them for being willing.

With this field of gratitude you're breaking free from your own egoic perception of separation, envy, jealousy, and all those things that's part of the human condition. Jealousy is wanting what someone else has. Envy is not wanting them to have what they have. Envy is jealousy on steroids! But it's a part of the egoic condition. However, you're celebrating somebody else's good now. You are projecting onto them what is within you, and you'll demonstrate abundance according to your own unique pattern. You can see that their abundance is making a way for others to break through.

Embrace what you see in them, and now embrace that vibration in yourself. If you can't see it because you can't recall it, again, use your imagination. What would that feel like? Someone has given us evidence of what it looks like in their life, and we applauded them. We've broken free from the ego's clutching that leads to jealousy and envy. We celebrate the good we see in another, now celebrate it in yourself. Feel the good in yourself. It's here. It's now. There's no shelf life, there's no expiration date on the good that's in you. This is a great manifestation exercise.

As you're embracing this within yourself right now, coupling it with that outrageous life you've already identified, you're now ready to birth something new in your life in this field of plenitude.

Say:

My choices are now operating from a field of plenitude!

My actions are now operating from a field of plenitude!

My generosity is now operating from a field of plenitude!

My giving is operating from a field of plenitude!

I am available to more good than I've ever imagined, manifested, or experienced before!

I am available to more prosperity than I've ever experienced, seen, or manifested before!

I am available to more wealth and well-being than I've ever experienced, realized, or manifested before!

It's happening right now!

It takes strength to buck the system. It takes strength to develop enough momentum to go beyond the inertia of the filters that have been holding you down. It takes strength to realize when you've been driving with your brakes on, now applaud yourself. Take a deep breath and shout, *"I am free!"* Take a deep breath and shout, *"I am prosperous!"* Take a deep breath and shout, *"I am willing to be prosperous! I am willing to be healthy! I am willing to be wealthy! I am willing to share! I am willing to be uplifted beyond my imagination!"* And every time you hear about something good happening for somebody, just inwardly give thanks for it. Say, *"Yes! That means there's possibilities for me! There's great possibilities for all of us!"*

You see, we're just creating a new space here. Prosperity, plenitude, and infinite possibilities is in tune with our soul purpose and mission. We all have the same purpose: to reflect and reveal the face of God, the face of the cosmos, in a way that it has never happened before. Our missions, however, will vary. We all have different ways of expressing that purpose. Some people are healers, musicians, choreographers, educators, teachers—we all have different ways of being.

Now while our purpose is all the same, the turbulence of the human condition, fraught with those thought-forms of separation, has us living mainly from a survival consciousness. And you sometimes just give up. You lose your purpose and you give up your mission just to survive. But now we want to come back to our purpose and mission. Even if we currently have employment that's not within our mission, that employment becomes the fuel and funding for our mission while we pay attention to our purpose and allow ourselves to be directed to what will order our steps.

Here's one final activation exercise. See yourself right now lying in your bed. You're waking up from a deep sleep. Your first tithe, your first offering in the morning is, *Thank you. I have another opportunity to live my purpose and to give my gifts.* This becomes a new set point when you wake up. Say,

> *"Thank you. I have another opportunity to live my purpose and to fulfill my mission. I am not entrained to the world's filters of lack, I am becoming in tune with the fundamental harmony of the Universe. The fundamental order of existence is governing my actions. I am walking with God, love, beauty, and abundance. My purpose will be fulfilled and there's nothing outside of me that can detour or hinder this. I am willing to be prosperous. I am willing to be*

51

happy. The possibilities are endless and limitless. I am recalibrating my mind to excellence. My focus is excellence. The turbulence of the human condition has less and less effect on me. I am willing to be happy."

Prosperity, plenitude, and infinite possibilities is happening in your life right now. If you're experiencing a challenge and you don't see how it can be resolved, the mind creates worst-case scenarios. It thinks, *what's the worst possible thing that could happen out of this?* But right now, whatever that thing is, begin to design your life by letting your mind go outside its present paradigm and think, *what is the best-case scenario for this thing in my life? What is the best possible thing that could occur? What is the great miracle that's awaiting me? What could possibly happen that could change this whole thing up? I am open to feeling, seeing, and catching it now. It's happened for others therefore it could happen for me. What is the best-case scenario?* Continue to expand this best-case scenario.

And now, we close with this prayer:

Infinite Presence, that which is closer to us than our breathing and nearer than our hands and feet, I am in perfect alignment with the absolute that is comparable to nothing, for it's all there is. In this moment of pure connection with the absolute Presence of the great power, the great love, the great joy, the great I AM of which all else is inference, I give great thanks and pure gratitude and thanksgiving that as I am lifted up into this spiritual atmosphere of the all good, I draw all men and women into this frequency of wholeness, vitalizing good, harmonizing prosperity, wealth, abundance, plenitude and well-being. And anything heretofore that would have hindered this is dissolved into the no-thingness from which it came, never to exist again. We stand free and available to more good than we have ever imagined, experienced, or manifested before. Something wonderful is happening through and as us right now in this field of living, loving intelligence. Everything is working together for our individual and collective good and we give thanks that this is so. I am grateful for this and let it be. And so it is. Amen.

Michael B. Beckwith

Michael B. Beckwith is the Founder and Spiritual Director of the Agape International Spiritual Center, a trans-denominational community headquartered in Los Angeles since 1986 and comprised  of thousands of local members and global live streamers. Highly regarded for his teachings on the science of inner transformation, Dr. Beckwith embraces a practical approach to spirituality utilizing meditation, affirmative prayer, and Life Visioning™, a process he originated. These practices teach us to take the experience of inner peace and awakened awareness into our everyday lives.

In 2012, Dr. Beckwith addressed the UN General Assembly during its annual World Interfaith Harmony Week. As co-founder and president of the Association for Global New Thought, he hosts conferences featuring harbingers of world peace including His Holiness the Dalai Lama, and had the distinguished honor of presenting to Nelson Mandela the Gandhi King Award.

Dr. Beckwith is a sought-after meditation teacher, conference speaker, and seminar leader on the Life Visioning Process™. Three of his books—*Life Visioning, Spiritual Liberation,* and *TranscenDance Expanded*—are recipients of the prestigious Nautilus Award. He has appeared on the Oprah Winfrey Network's SuperSoul Sunday, SuperSoul Sessions, and Help Desk; Dr. Oz; CNN, The Oprah Show; Larry King Live; Tavis Smiley; and in his own PBS Special, The Answer Is You, and is a member of Oprah's prestigious inaugural SuperSoul 100. Every Friday at 1pm PST, thousands tune into his radio show on KPFK, WAKE UP! The Sound of Transformation.

For more information visit:

www.agapelive.com and www.michaelbeckwith. com

Also by Michael B. Beckwith

Spiritual Liberation: Fulfilling Your Soul's Potential

Life Visioning: A Transformative Process for Activating Your Unique Gifts and Highest Potential

TranscenDance Expanded

The Answer Is You: Heart Sets and Mind Sets For Self-Discovery

40 Day Mind Fast Soul Feast: A Guide to Soul Awakening and Inner Fulfillment

A Manifesto Of Peace: Light on the Path of an Emissary of Peace

Journal

Made in the USA
San Bernardino, CA
19 February 2020